THE BOY AND THE BATTLE

A READ ALOUD BIBLE STORY BOOK FOR KIDS – THE STORY OF DAVID AND GOLIATH, RETOLD FOR BEGINNERS

JENNIFER CARTER

D1714777

Illustrated by
HATTIE MILLIDGE

INTRODUCTION

This is a story about a young boy called David.

It's a re-imagining of the Bible story which is told in 1 Samuel, chapters 16 and 17.

As you're listening, remember that this story is part of history.

It really did happen.

THE GIANT AND THE BATTLEFIELD

On the battlefield stood a giant of a man. He was impossibly tall. His bronze helmet and armor gleamed in the sunlight. Beside him, dwarfed in his shadow, stood his armor bearer.

The giants' voice bellowed out across the valley. "Why do you come out and line up for battle? Choose a man to fight me! If he's able to fight and kill me, the Philistines will be your slaves. But if I win the fight and kill him, you'll become our slaves and serve us. Choose your man and let's fight!"

The Israelite army, to a man, trembled. Every day, for forty days, this giant of a man had come forward. Every morning and every evening, he'd shouted out the same challenge.

But who among them could stand up to such an enemy? Who among them could take on their shoulders such a responsibility? Most important of all, who among them could possibly fight him and win?

They didn't know it, but today was different. Hidden among the ranks of the army, was a young boy. His father had sent him to take food for his brothers, who'd been on the battlefield for several weeks.

But this was no ordinary young boy. Although no-one was expecting it, he was about to do something quite impossibly amazing.

But we're starting in the middle of the story. So, let's go back to the beginning and tell you more about this boy and just who he was.

2

THE SHEPHERD BOY

Jesse was a good father. He had eight sons and, like any good father, he was immensely proud of each one of them.

One thing Jesse loved was to tell his sons stories. He often told them the story of his beloved grandparents.

"One day, my grandfather, a landowner, showed kindness to a poor widow in the fields. He allowed her to collect the grain left after the harvest. This young woman had a kind heart. She was looking after her mother-in-law, and had been since her husband died.

My grandfather was a kind man. He made sure

that this young widow was not bullied or treated badly by the workers in his fields.

Although it started with a simple act of kindness, the story ended with my grandfather inviting the young widow to become his wife."

Jesse also told his boys stories about their people, the Israelites, and the God who'd saved them from slavery in Egypt.

David, Jesse's youngest son, loved listening to his father's stories. As the youngest son, he was often sent into the hills to look after the sheep.

It wasn't a glamorous job, and he was often lonely, but he loved what he did. Although he missed being with his family, he loved being out in the open air, and spending time with his sheep.

With nothing but the moon and stars for company, David would think about the stories his father told.

He thought about the God who created the hills, the stars and the wide blue sky. He remembered the stories he'd heard about this God who rescued His people. And he wondered what this God might do next.

David could often be seen practicing with his sling and stones. He wanted to be ready to scare off any wild animals that might threaten his sheep. He knew that his father trusted him to keep the sheep safe.

On many a moonlit night, David could be seen playing his harp, with only sheep for an audience. He loved to sing and would often make up songs, that spoke about the God of his people.

David grew to trust this God that he'd heard his father talk about. He trusted Him to help him keep his flock safe from the lions and bears that prowled the hills around him.

With no-one but his sheep to talk to, David would often find himself talking to God. When he begun to think about the dangers in the surrounding hill country, David found that singing songs or talking with God would calm his heart.

AT HOME IN BETHLEHEM

Back at David's home in Bethlehem, something unusual was happening. Someone special was arriving. The prophet Samuel had come to visit their small town.

The word spread quickly in the village. This was indeed an honor, but the elders of the town welcomed him nervously. They wondered what had brought him to their village. Was it good news, or bad?

"I come in peace," Samuel said.

At these words, the tension disappeared and worried frowns were replaced by smiles.

They may not have felt so relaxed, if they'd

known that the prophet Samuel was on a special mission. He'd been sent there by God.

Although God had been speaking to King Saul, the King refused to listen. King Saul had been his own way for many years.

Finally, God had spoken to Samuel. He told Samuel it was time to choose a new king.

He'd sent Samuel to the small town of Bethlehem to choose one of Jesse's sons to be king. No-one else knew of the prophet's secret mission.

Samuel, the prophet, asked Jesse to bring all his sons to meet him. Then he asked that each of the sons might pass in front of him.

The first boy passed in front of Samuel. He was tall and good-looking. He looked like sort of person you might imagine growing to be a King.

But God said to Samuel. "Don't think about his appearance or height. I don't look at the things that people look at. People look at the outward appearance, but I look at their heart."

Another son passed in front of Samuel. "I have not chosen this one either", God whispered.

Seven of Jesse's sons passed before Samuel, but

each time Samuel said, "The Lord has not chosen this one."

Finally, every one of Jesse's sons had passed before Samuel. Perplexed, he asked, " Are these all your sons?"

"My youngest son is out on the hills, looking after the sheep," replied Jesse.

"Send for him. We'll wait here until he comes," said Samuel.

Jesse sent a messenger, urging him to bring David home quickly. It wasn't long until David came running in.

Samuel could see how handsome and strong he was, but he remembered what God had said about looking at the heart, not the outward appearance. So, he waited and listened.

Then he heard God say to him, "Rise and anoint him, he is the one."

So, Samuel took some oil and, with all the brothers watching, David, the youngest son, was anointed king.

It would take many years before David would be recognized as king over Israel. There would be battles to fight, and challenges to overcome. But from that day, David knew that God was with him. He could sense God empowering him for what lay ahead.

For now, he remained a simple shepherd boy, who had been anointed to be King. He returned to the hills and his sheep, while his brothers wondered about all that had happened that day.

4

IN THE COURT OF THE KING

In the courts of King Saul, his advisers were worried. The King was in a very dark mood, and nothing could shake him out of it. They tried all sorts of things, but nothing seemed to make a difference.

Finally, someone had an idea. " What about music?" they suggested. It was agreed that one of his trusted advisors would ask the king.

"Shall we send for a musician? Someone who can play for you, help to quiet and calm your mind?" they asked.

King Saul seemed to like this idea. "Yes, find someone who plays well and bring him to me," he replied.

The king's advisers were so happy. Now there was something they could do to help the King. But who could they send for? Who could play the kind of music that could break the dark cloud hanging over their King?

As they were worrying and discussing this, a servant who'd just come into the room spoke up. "I know someone. It's Jesse's son. He's from Bethlehem. He sings and plays beautifully and God is with him. He's a good-looking boy and he really knows how to handle a weapon."

At once, the advisors sent messengers from the Palace to Jesse's home, with a message from the King, " Send me your son, David". And so it was that David came to the Palace.

He played for the King, and the King was very pleased, and the advisers were happy. For whenever the dark mood would come on the King, David would bring his harp and play beautiful music. As David played, it would calm the King's mind and his dark mood would leave him.

It wasn't long until King Saul asked Jesse if David could remain in the Palace.

The King had learnt to trust David. He knew he'd

stand by him in times of danger. So, even though David was still a boy, he appointed David as one of his armor bearer's. It was a great honor for anyone, let alone a shepherd boy from Bethlehem.

5

GATHERING FOR WAR

For a time there was peace in the land, but it didn't last long.

News reached the palace that their enemies, the Philistines, were gathering and preparing for war.

It was time for the nation to prepare for battle. King Saul began to gather his army, ready to fight against the Philistines.

As he was only a boy, David left the palace and returned home to his father, who needed him to care for the sheep.

When he arrived home, David found his three eldest brothers preparing to leave for the battle lines. They were keen to fight in the Israelite army.

It was a long march for his brothers to reach the valley where the Philistine army had assembled. This was where battle would take place and history would be made.

As the Israelite fighting men arrived, they saw the Philistines lined up on the other side of the valley. They set up their camp, with just the valley between the two armies.

Back home, Jesse was waiting for news about his sons on the battlefield. After waiting for weeks without news, he sent David to the frontline, with a gift of bread for his brothers and some cheese for their commanding officer.

"See how your brothers are," he asked, "and bring me back a message from them."

Leaving his sheep in the care of another shepherd, David did as his father asked. Leaving early in the morning, he reached the camp as it was in turmoil.

The army was moving into battle positions, shouting the loud war cry at their enemies across the valley. The ground shook beneath their feet, as with their stamping feet and loud cries, the army marched forward.

Suddenly, a hush fell. David continued to make his way between the men, searching for the familiar faces of his brothers. Then, he looked across the valley. One of the Philistines, a giant of a man, stepped forward from the battle lines, striding out towards the Israelites battle lines.

He heard the men speaking in hushed voices, "See how he defies us. The King has promised great riches to the Israelite warrior who kills this man. He'll even give him his daughter's hand in marriage."

David interrupted them, "Who is this who defies the armies of the living God?" he asked.

The men were astonished. What kind of a question was this for a boy to be asking?

Just as he was asking this question, the giant began to shout. "Choose someone to fight me," he roared. "Send a man and let us fight." He taunted them defiantly.

This giant of a man was the Philistine champion. He stood head and shoulders taller than any man on either side of the valley.

At the giant's words, the strong lines of the

Israelite army seemed to dissolve. Some ran in fear. Others hurriedly made their way back to camp.

Among the retreating soldiers, David picked out some familiar faces. His brothers, at last! Running up to them, he handed them the gifts from their father.

"Why did you bother coming here?" asked his brother angrily. "You're such a selfish boy. Did you leave the sheep on the hills to die, just so you could watch the battle?"

David's brothers had been jealous of him, ever since the day that the prophet had come to their house. They couldn't forgive him for being the one Samuel chose, instead of them.

Walking up to another group of soldiers, David asked, "What will be done for the man who kills this giant? Who is he that he defies the armies of the living God?"

They answered him, the same as the other men, "The king will give great riches, and his daughter's hand in marriage, to the man who defeats him."

It wasn't long until the story of Davids' question reached the ears of the King. He summoned

David to his tent, eager to see the boy who asked such a question.

David walked calmly into the King's tent and said, "Don't lose heart. I will go and fight this giant."

"But you're just a boy," the King replied. "Goliath has been the Philistines champion for many years."

David looked up at the King and spoke calmly. "When I looked after my father's sheep, a lion or a bear came to carry away the sheep from the flock. I chased them and rescued the sheep. I have killed both lion and bear, and I will kill this man too, because he has defied the armies of the living God. My God, who kept me safe from the wild beasts in the desert, will keep me safe from this wild beast in the valley."

"Go then, and God be with you," replied King Saul, giving his blessing.

The advisers were astonished. They knew that the battle would determine the future of their entire nation. They could hardly believe that the King would give such responsibility to someone who wasn't even a real soldier, he was just a boy.

THE BOY AND THE BATTLE

Saul called for his armor to be brought for David and insisted that David try it on.

At King Saul's orders, the men put the coat of armor on David, placed the bronze helmet on his head and fastened the King's sword to his belt.

David tried to take a few steps, but it was impossible. The armor was too heavy. He couldn't move.

"I can't fight in these," he said to Saul. "I'm not used to them."

So David took off the King's armor. Taking his shepherd's staff in his hand, he walked down to a nearby stream. Slowly, carefully, he picked out five smooth stones.

Rolling them in his hand, warming them in the heat of the sun, he gently placed each one in his shepherd's pouch.

Without saying a word, David strode forward into the valley. He could feel every eye on him. Watching. Waiting. Wondering.

The Philistines champion saw him and walked out towards him. This giant was towering into the sky and laughing.

"Am I dog, that you come at me with a stick? I'll soon be feeding you to the birds and the beasts," he laughed.

But David stood still, looking the giant right in the eye. Then he spoke.

" You come to fight me with sword, spear and javelin. I come to fight you as a servant of the living God. He is God of the army of Israel. He is the God you have defied.

Today I will kill you. It will be you and the Philistine armies that are fed to the birds and beasts today. This battle is not mine, but God's. It is the God of Israel that will help me win this battle."

Without taking his eyes away from the giant, David gently reached into his pouch. He drew out one smooth stone.

His heart was pounding within him, but he remembered the words to one of his own songs, "When I am afraid, I will trust in you".

"Yes, I'll trust in you," he thought to himself as he began to run. Not away from this giant of a man, but towards him.

Looking carefully at his target, he placed the smooth stone into the sling. Then he swung the sling and the stone above his head.

As he let go, the stone launched itself at the towering giant standing before him. Time seemed to stand still.

The stone flew across the air. Every fighting man held his breath. Waiting. Watching.

The stone found it's target, hitting the giant on his forehead. Sinking in. A look of surprise flashed across his face and then was gone. The giant sank to his knees and fell, with his face to the ground.

For a moment, David was quiet, as his heart thanked God. Once again his God had given him strength to defeat a wild beast.

Then it was time for action. He ran forward to the slumped body of the giant. Heaving Goliath's sword from its scabbard, with one blow, he cut off the giant's head.

As he did so, he heard a sound he couldn't place. He looked up at the hillside before him. The Philistine army were running. They were running away up the hill, away from the scene of their defeat.

At that exact moment, a deafening roar came from behind him. David turned to see the entire Israelite army cheering.

They couldn't believe that the battle was won, without one of them having to draw his sword. They were waving their hands, swords and shields, each man roaring "Victory!" at the sight of their retreating enemy.

As one man, the army charged forward. David watched, as the army ran.

He remembered how God had helped him kill wild animals on the hillside. David knew that without God giving him strength, it could have been Israelite army who were the ones running away.

David felt exhausted. He didn't know how long

he'd been standing there, until a man he recognized from the king's court approached him. "The king wants to see you".

He was still holding Goliath's head in his hand, as he came into the King's tent.

Here he was, a simple shepherd boy, standing before the king. He'd defeated their enemy with a single stone. From being a shepherd boy in the hills, he'd come to the battlefield, and now, here he was in the presence of the King.

"David, I've decided that you must come and stay in my house. What you've done today has shown great courage. " King Saul announced.

Jonathan, the King's son was standing nearby. He took off the robe he was wearing and gave it to David. Then he took off his sword, belt and his bow, and gave them to David.

Everyone watching was amazed.This was such an honor and mark of respect, from the King's son himself.

They didn't know it yet, but Jonathan and David would become firm friends. They'd be like brothers, sharing many adventures with each other.

From that day on, whatever Saul sent him to do,

David did. As promised, he married the King's daughter. He became a hero in the land, with women singing songs about him and how he'd killed the giant, Goliath.

Yet David knew the truth. It wasn't really him who'd killed Goliath and defeated the Philistine army.

It was the same God who'd helped him defeat the lion and the bear on the hillside, that was with him on the battlefield.

David would go on to have many more adventures with God. His journey would not be easy.

One day, he would become King of Israel. He'd be a wise King and be much loved by his people.

EPILOGUE

David learned to trust God while he was all alone on a hillside, looking after the sheep.

It took many years for David to become the strong and courageous boy who faced a giant and won.

He'd learned to trust God, even when he was afraid. He learned that God could help him be strong, even when he felt weak.

David wasn't expecting a battle when he took the loaves of bread to his brothers. Yet God had been preparing him in the wilderness, when he was looking after the sheep.

David fought many small battles, long before he fought against Goliath.

He fought fear when the bear and the lion came to steal away his sheep. He fought against loneliness on the hillside with the sheep. He fought the spears and arrows of his brother's unkind words.

In those quiet moments on the hillside, he'd learned to hear God's voice and grew to trust Him.

When David grew to be a man, he didn't always get things right. But he knew that there was someone he could turn to when things went wrong.

A DIFFERENT STORY

You can find a hero like David in the New Testament. His name is Jesus. He was an unlikely hero too.

Jesus won a different battle. A battle with death itself.

You can read about his battle in the Bible or listen to the story, **The Big Catch of Fish**, by the same author.

A Christmas Surprise, tells the story of the very first Christmas and how Jesus arrived in this world as a baby.

Rediscover the Christmas story through four short

stories that look at the story of the birth of baby Jesus - as seen by the donkey in the stable, the shepherds on a hillside, the star gazing down on the little town of Bethlehem, and the baby's mother, Mary.

GET THE FREE AUDIOBOOK

You can download the audiobook, read by Rod Johnson, for free. (This offer does not apply to existing Audible subscribers)

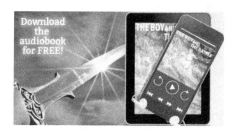

Go to getbook.at/goliath to download your FREE audiobook

What listeners are saying:

"Be strengthened by the story of faith and grit".

"Delightful, engaging and memorable"

CPSIA information can be obtained
at www.ICGtesting.com
Printed in the USA
BVHW041337230721
612717BV00012B/610

9 781908 567185